Monica:
A Prodigal's Praying Mother

Monica

A Prodigal's Praying Mother

by
George W. Rice

Beacon Hill Press of Kansas City
Kansas City, Missouri

Copyright 1989 by
Beacon Hill Press of Kansas City

ISBN: 083-411-2868

Printed in the
United States of America

Cover Art: Crandall Vail

10   9   8   7   6   5   4   3   2

Contents

Introduction

Monica: A Prodigal's Praying Mother is the story of the mother of the man known as Augustine. Her prayers and godly example were the chief means used of God to bring about his salvation and to prepare him for his outstanding life of service to God and His Church. The author's prayer is that it will challenge all parents who read this to set a similar example before their children, and that it will also encourage their efforts to see every one of their family, by God's amazing grace, brought to a saving knowledge of Jesus Christ.

Someone has said that "behind every great man stands a great woman." This was never more true than in the case of Augustine, who lived from A.D. 354 to 430. He was tremendously influential in his own day, becoming the greatest of the Early Church fathers, and later was canonized by his denomination. The entire Church of Jesus Christ, of all branches, centuries, and cultures, is deeply indebted to him for his clear doctrinal expression of biblical truth. Perhaps his greatest contribution was his emphasis on the doctrine that "there is no power but divine grace, as revealed in the life and death of the Son of God, that could bring rest to human weariness, or pardon and peace for human guilt."

Augustine is best remembered for his *Confessions,* a collection of 13 books describing his spiritual journey from sinner to saint. This devotional classic reveals the devoutness and aspirations of a great soul. *Monica: A Prodigal's Praying Mother* is based largely on these *Confessions.*

—GWR

1. *Family Background*

"I lied to my mother" was Augustine's confession many years after the actual fact. It was not just that he had lied that brought his heart to penitential tears. He had committed many more gross and hurtful sins during his years as a far-country prodigal. It was rather that he had deceived his beloved mother. "And such a mother" was his added description of Monica, a humble housewife of the ancient town of Tagaste in North Africa.

Monica had been reared in a godly home. Her father was a faithful Christian and an active member of his church. But her parents, for whatever reasons, turned over to others the major responsibility of rearing Monica and her sisters. Their greatest training came from a devoted household servant, who lovingly cared for all the children with unusual wisdom and discipline.

A wife of noble character who can find? . . . Her children arise and call her blessed.   PROV. 31:10, 28

Today's alcohol and drug problems of children and youth are not limited to our own era. Augustine tells of one situation that reveals Monica's devotion and sensitivity to God, even as a young girl. She lived in a century and an area where wine was a part of most adult meals. Her daily household chore was the task of drawing the liquor from a basement cask. Not realizing the subtle power of little things, and before she realized its danger, there had stolen upon her a love of wine. She would wet her lips each day as she filled the pitcher with the liquor. Her teenage desires intensified until she began to carry along a little cup when she went to the cellar, from which she drank eagerly and increasingly. Fortunately, however, a maidservant detected her secret addiction and taunted her as a "winebibber." Rather than denying or justifying her habit, Monica "perceived her foulness and immediately condemned and renounced it." Undoubtedly she later used the memory of this experience as a warning to her son, for with all his other later vices, he never became a drunkard.

Do not gaze at wine when it is red, when it sparkles in the cup, when it goes down smoothly! In the end it bites like a snake and poisons like a viper.　　　PROV. 23:31-32

Monica must have known the biblical exhortation to "be not drunk with wine, wherein is excess; but be filled with the Spirit" (Eph. 5:18, KJV). God was preparing her, as He seeks to do with every child and youth, for her vital role as a responsible parent in the years ahead.

Augustine gives God the major credit for preparing Monica to become such an outstanding mother. Somewhere in her youth, she developed the kind of relationship with God that helped her to graciously submit to the guidance of her parents and teachers. This also was preparation for her later remarkable ministry of intercessory prayer for the salvation of her family.

In the custom of that century, when Monica reached marriageable age, she was given to a husband. Patricius proved to be anything but an ideal companion, even violating his marriage vows. He did little to control his vile temper, often becoming violent in fits of anger, especially when he was drinking heavily. The young wife had love for him tough enough to face his shortcomings but wise enough to know when best to do this. She consistently "busied herself to gain him to God, preaching Christ unto him by her behavior." Though this process took 20 long years, she never gave up.

Patricius was nominally religious but lived the life-style of his pagan neighbors. Centuries before today's liberated women would become partners with their husbands in making family decisions, Monica's godly submission and wisdom impressed her growing boy. He declared that his father never overcame the influence of his mother's piety on his young life.

In patience and meekness she likewise "conquered by submission" her mother-in-law, and they lived together "with a wonderful sweetness of mutual goodwill."

Augustine recognized that, even in this potentially volatile area, God had been Monica's "most intimate instructor, teaching her in the school of her heart." All of her pastors, whom she revered as God's servants, also recognized God's presence in her heart because of her fruitful, holy living. As her son would later record, her faithfulness and devotion caused them to "magnify, honor, and love God."

Submit to one another out of reverence for Christ. Wives, submit to your husbands as to the Lord. . . . Husbands, love your wives, just as Christ loved the church and gave himself up for her.
EPH. 5:21-22, 25

2. *Home Training*

Monica was unquestionably a model Christian mother. She did her best to teach her talented son the truths of Scripture as interpreted by her church. Augustine would later testify that "this name of my Savior was treasured even with my mother's milk." In his later worst years, he could not forget the teaching of the reality of eternal life "through the humility of the Lord our God" (see Phil. 2:5-11). Nor did she depend upon home training alone, but, as he testifies, "I was brought to the church even from the womb of my mother, who greatly trusted in Thee."

As a young boy, Augustine became very ill and soon was at the point of death. As he pictured it, his troubled mother, "with a heart pure in Thy faith," prayed with desperate intensity. He confesses that at this time, "I believed with my mother and my whole house, except my father." He re-

---

Train a child in the way he should go, and when he is old he will not turn from it.   PROV. 22:6

quested baptism, but his father, not yet a Christian himself, was reluctant to give his consent. His mother may have thought him too young to be ready to express such personal faith in her Savior. Or she may have yielded to the chauvinistic submission demanded by husbands in that ancient day.

Even as a child, Augustine was considered by his teachers as "a boy of good promise." As he later evaluated himself, "I had learned to take pleasure in truth. I was averse to being deceived, I had a vigorous memory, was provided with the power of speech, was softened by friendship, and shunned sorrow, meanness, and ignorance." Monica must have taken great delight in seeing him grow up to love God and His Church.

Her son would, however, gently chide his mother for following too closely the permissive attitude of her day. He could have wished that his parents had kept a tighter rein on his associates and activities. The negative effects of his divided home influences showed up by his middle teen years. Like the New Testament prodigal, he for-

---

Everyone who heard this wondered about it, asking, "What then is this child going to be?" For the Lord's hand was with him.   LUKE 1:66

sook the "delights of God's house" and plunged into the far country, in "the madness of sexual lust." Like too many modern prodigals, Augustine cherished his mother's ideals but followed his father's example.

Augustine's only criticism of his parents was that both of them, with differing motivation, were "too anxious that he should acquire much learning." His father was eager for his son to be trained in whatever occupation would bring fortune and fame. His mother had the mistaken idea that this higher education might help lead him to her Savior. Patricius was just a poor laborer, but he and Monica sacrificed to enroll their son in an oratorical school. Just as in most secular schools in this generation, his teachers were basically indifferent about his spiritual life and moral behavior. Their task, as they saw it, was to train him not to make a life but to make a living. Their only concern was that he should learn to make a powerful speech and become a persuasive orator.

Augustine seemed to be a natural-born leader. This strength, however, became his weakness. As he pictures it, "I longed in my youth to be satisfied with worldly things, and became corrupt in God's eyes, pleasing myself, and eager to please in the eyes of men."

He soon followed the path of the New Testament prodigal, even while still living under his mother's roof. As he later described his actions, "It is not by our feet, nor by change of place, that we either turn from God or return to Him." Far country distance from God is to be measured not in kilometers but in moral miles.

His superior intelligence became a fountain of pride that brought about his spiritual downfall. He became, as he described it, "too smart for the Scriptures." He scorned his childhood teachings and, "swollen with pride, looked upon myself as a great one." He refused to humble himself "under God's mighty hand," forgetting that "God opposes the proud but gives grace to the humble" (1 Pet. 5:6, 5). His arrogant mind still could not reach the inner meaning of the New Testament, and he became too proud to admit his need of God's help or guidance.

He later confessed that "I sank away from You, O God, and I wandered too far from You in my youth." Again, "It [evil] was foul, and I loved it. I loved to perish." He became proud of what should have shamed him. As he began to take

---

Pride goes before destruction, a haughty spirit before a fall. Better to be lowly in spirit and among the oppressed than to share plunder with the proud.   PROV. 16:18-19

16

leadership in sinning, he pictured himself to his friends as being worse than he actually was, for "among my equals I was ashamed to be less shameless." He chose low companions and would later confess that "in all this there was a mist, shutting out from my sight the fullness of Thy truth, O my God." In the same way that spiritual rebellion affects youth today, his sin had hidden God's face.

During these difficult years, when a lesser soul might have given up in despair, Monica faithfully prayed, both for her unsaved spouse and their rebellious boy. She had the great joy of seeing Patricius, her husband, become a seeker, a believer, and finally a baptized member of her church. It was just in time, for he died within a year after making his profession of faith. All this only intensified the widow's prayers and efforts to see her erring son reached with the gospel of Christ. As he described her feelings, "She feared those crooked paths in which they walk who turn their back to God, and not their face."

———————

God has called us to live in peace. How do you know, wife, whether you will save your husband?   1 COR. 7:15-16

3. *Throwing Off Restraint*

Early in his university years, Augustine became involved with a mistress, who bore him an illegitimate son, named Adeodatus. Modeling what too many moderns have ignorantly called "new morality," he left his mother's home and moved in with this woman.

One can only imagine his mother's distress. Monica was not concerned with what this disgrace would do to her own reputation but thought only of his eternal welfare. She never rejected her son but in love accepted him even when she deeply disapproved of his actions and attitudes. His own genuine love and respect for her made him tolerate her persistent "nagging" appeals.

Like many modern university sophisticates, Augustine then joined a popular cult, whose teaching supported his "liberated" life-style. This Manichaean group was amazingly like several so-called modern heresies. His love for what he later described as "vagrant liberty" sounds like the determination of too many modern young people to "do their own thing." They should listen to his penetrating analysis: "Such was my life. But was it life, O my God?"

Augustine's mother never gave up. As her boy's interest in God and the church decreased, her prayers increased. He confesses later, "That pure and prudent widow twice a day came to the church without intermission in order that she might listen to God in His sermons, and God might listen to her in her prayers." For too many long, discouraging years, those prayers had little apparent effect. But she just kept on praying and believing.

Monica knew little of Augustine's new cultish beliefs. She could not reach him intellectually. She pleaded with a visiting bishop to, in Augustine's words, "talk with me, refute my errors, unteach me evil things, and teach me good." This priest, who had himself been delivered from the domination of the same cult, advised that her son "was still unteachable, being inflated with the novelty of that heresy." Then he told her, "Just leave him alone for a time." He encouraged her to keep on praying and to cease nagging him until

----

As for me, far be it from me that I should sin against the Lord by failing to pray for you. And I will teach you the way that is good and right.   1 SAM. 12:23

her son, by his own reading and reasoning, would discover how great was his sinful error.

Monica could not accept this and continued to press him to deal with her beloved prodigal. A little vexed with her persistent pleading, he exclaimed, "Go thy way, and God bless you, for it is not possible that the son of these tears should perish." She accepted this as though it were God's voice from heaven, and often mentioned the assurance to her stubborn, apparently unresponsive son.

Augustine rapidly gained a growing reputation as an outstanding teacher of language and oratory. His moral journey, however, was all downhill. As he later deplored, "For nearly nine years I wallowed in the slime of that deep pit and the darkness of falsehood, striving often to rise, but being all the more heavily dashed down." It is to Augustine's credit that he never glamorized his sinful attitudes and activities. Even in the midst of his indecision, he was like the late hymn writer William J. Kirkpatrick, who penned, "I've wasted many precious years." But he was not yet persuaded to come home to his waiting Heavenly Father or to respond to his praying mother.

Commit your way to the Lord; trust in him and he will do [it].
PS. 37:5

Meanwhile, as he later testified, "My mother, God's faithful one, wept to God on my behalf more than mothers are wont to weep the bodily deaths of their children." Her tears "watered the earth under her eyes in every place where she prayed." God did not allow her to carry her burden of intercession without His blessing. Sometime during this tragic period, Monica "prayed clear through." God confirmed in her heart the assurance that her prodigal would finally be saved from his sins.

This inner witness only intensified her intercession for him. As he later declared, "That chaste, pious, and sober widow," now buoyed up with this hope, prayed harder and longer. Her son was still reacting against God's efforts to reach him; just like Saul on the Damascus road, he still did "kick against the goads" (Acts 26:14). Augustine appreciated those fervent prayers and knew that they entered into God's presence, even though he was, as he describes it, still "involved and reinvolved in that darkness."

This is the confidence we have in approaching God: that if we ask anything according to his will, he hears us. And if we know that he hears us—whatever we ask—we know that we have what we asked of him.   1 JOHN 5:14-15

4. *Disillusionment with False Teaching*

About this time, Augustine spent some time with Faustus, the chief guru of the Manichaean cult. He found this man to be an eloquent speaker, which greatly appealed to the young teacher of oratory. But the cultish leader could not, and would not even try to, answer his persistent questions. Augustine did respect his leader's apparent sincerity and humility. But he reacted against the efforts of this "cult of personality worship" to control his questioning mind. This close association with Faustus disillusioned him and, as he admits, "began to loosen the snare in which I had been taken."

Augustine now became increasingly disenchanted with his total support group. In his own words, "I sought for pleasures, honors, and truths, thereby falling into sorrows, troubles, and errors." His strong, logical mind finally helped him to see through the shallowness and inconsistencies of his cultish teaching and leadership. He still retained, however, their depraved ideas about God, sin, and salvation. He could not accept the truth that "the Word became flesh" in Christ (John 1:14). His cult had taught him that human flesh was tied in with eternal wickedness. As he writes, "I was afraid to believe Jesus to be born in the flesh, lest I should be compelled to believe Him contaminated by the flesh." God, however, was still working to answer Monica's prayers for her confused son.

About this time, the proud young intellectual missed another great opportunity to "draw near to God" (Heb. 10:22). Seeking to justify his own increasingly depraved life-style, he led a close friend away from the truth, as he described the process, "into the same superstitions and pernicious fables which my mother mourned in me." This friend contracted what proved to be a fatal fever and was then baptized. When Augustine tried to make a mocking joke with him about the rite, "he shuddered at me, as if I were his enemy." In a short while his friend died, still clinging to his faith in Christ. The young teacher was devastated in his

---

The word of God is living and active. Sharper than any double-edged sword, . . . it judges the thoughts and attitudes of the heart. HEB. 4:12

sorrow, and as he describes it, he "bore about with him a battered and bleeding soul." His cultish belief made God but an empty phantasm, not worthy of worship. So he turned back to the beggarly elements of the world. Unfortunately, many friends were there to help him drown his sorrow in more licentious living. He could find mental rest only in bitterness.

Augustine was already discovering that God's gifts to man do not satisfy, but only God himself. As he would later express, in perhaps the most famous phrase from his *Confessions:* "You have made us for yourself, O God, and our hearts are restless till they find rest in You."

Now 31 years of age, Augustine was yet strongly enslaved by intellectual pride and physical sin, far from repentance and from God. In his barren restlessness, he decided to move away from his sometimes nagging, always praying mother. When he received an offer to teach rhetoric in Italy, he decided to move from his native North Africa to Rome, the capital city of the empire.

Where can I go . . . from your presence? . . . If I rise on the wings of the dawn, if I settle on the far side of the sea, even there your hand will guide me [and] hold me.

PS. 139:7, 9–10

Monica knew all too well that Rome was a moral cesspool in that ancient day. She feared that such a move would defeat her prayers and high hopes for her son and "grievously lamented my journey." "She violently restrained me," he wrote, and urgently insisted that he should give up his plans to leave their city of Carthage, in North Africa, or at least take her along with him to Rome. To avoid a painful confrontation, Augustine deceived her about his departure time and sailed north toward Rome, taking along his mistress and their teenage son.

Monica was devastated, "wild with grief." But she was "not backward in prayers and weeping." Her love was "tough enough" to strongly "accuse his cruelty and lack of honesty." Then she took up her daily cross of intercession for her headstrong boy. Augustine would later confess that "I cannot sufficiently express the love she had for me, nor how she now travailed for me in the spirit with a far keener anguish than when she bore me in the flesh."

The Spirit helps us in our weakness. We do not know what we ought to pray for, but the Spirit himself intercedes for us. ROM. 8:26

She had prayed so much that her boy would not go to Rome. But he had trampled over those prayers and lied to her in the process. That son would later explain, in his famous *Confessions,* that "like all mothers, she loved to have me with her, but knew not what joy God was preparing for her by my absence." Like ancient Joseph's enslaved trip to Egypt, God wanted this wayward youth to go to Rome. Augustine traveled there to satisfy his own selfish ambitions, but God was doing His work in all of these events to answer Monica's heart cry. God certainly denied her petition but answered her prayer, as an object lesson for prayer warriors of every generation, including our own time.

Augustine contracted a fever soon after arriving in Rome and was sick unto death. But this alone did not convince his mind or soften his heart toward God. He continued to excuse his wrongdoing and admits that his "sin was all the more incurable in that I did not deem myself a sinner."

God was urgently trying to get to the sick prodigal, but, as he later came to realize, "by the voices of my own errors was I driven forth, and by the weight of my own pride was I sinking into the lowest pit." His enormous pride had led him to believe that he could control his own destiny and stop any downward pull whenever he chose to do so. But now he felt the full weight of the chains his sinful habits had forged.

He did, however, begin to question the values for which he had lived so many wasted years. He realized the emptiness of everything he was living for. As he described his condition, "What did it profit me that I, the base slave of vile affections, read unaided and understood all the books that I could get of the so-called liberal arts?" He was a well-educated pagan but a slave to sin and vile affections. Yet he continued to justify himself and his licentious life-style.

Augustine was like the ancient Jews described by the apostle Paul: "Since they did not know the righteousness that comes from God and sought to establish their own, they did not submit to God's righteousness" (Rom. 10:3).

There in Rome, Augustine, the outstanding speaker and teacher of oratory, was drawn back to church. He still sat "in the seat of the scornful" (Ps. 1:1, KJV). As he describes his attitude, "I was but a careless, contemptuous spectator." He went initially just to hear an eloquent preacher. But he

---

What good will it be for a man if he gains the whole world, yet forfeits his soul? Or what can a man give in exchange for his soul?   MATT. 16:26

found that, in his own words, "While I opened my heart to admit 'How skillfully he spake,' there also entered with it, but gradually, 'And how truly he spake.'" Augustine could identify with those responding to the preacher of Goldsmith's classic, *The Deserted Village,*

> *Truth from his lips prevailed with double sway,*
> *And fools, who came to scoff, remained to pray.*

Bishop Ambrose received the young rebel with "a benevolent and episcopal kindliness." He won the young rebel to himself that he might then lead him to faith in Christ. Augustine says that "I began to love him, not at first indeed as a teacher of the truth—which I entirely despaired of in God's Church—but as a man friendly to myself." He was able to discuss his honest intellectual questions with this devout man of God. He started to study the New Testament, finally realizing that no man is strong enough by reason alone to find out the truth and for this cause all need the authority of the Holy Scriptures. He was almost surprised to find that "the gospel" was truly "the power of God unto salvation" (Rom. 1:16, KJV). God's claim on his life finally made sense to the scholarly youth, and he began to be brought under deep conviction of his spiritual need. Repentance and faith, however, did not come easily.

He had been strongly influenced by the agnosticism of certain philosophers, who prided themselves in "doubting everything and fluctuating between all." Here his solid training from childhood saved him from this fatal error. As he explains it, "Because they were without the saving name of Christ, I utterly refused to commit the care of my fainting soul to them." He finally decided to become a catechumen, a learner, "in the church my parents had commended to me, until something settled should manifest itself to me, whither I might steer my course." He admits that he would not have believed the gospel unless the church had persuaded him. In this he showed more wisdom than many erring moderns, who refuse to give God and His Church a chance to help them be healed of sin's wounds.

In his early rejection of the faith of his fathers, Augustine had also fallen an easy victim of the astrology practiced by the Manichaean culture of his day. He became enamored, like too many gullible moderns, with horoscopes and the signs of the zodiac, along with the influence of the var-

---

When you received the word of God . . . you accepted it . . . as it actually is, the word of God, which is at work in you who believe.   1 THESS. 2:13

ious constellations and stars on his decisions and circumstances. Unlike too many present-day horoscope devotees, he was finally convinced that he should "repudiate the lying divinations and impious absurdities of the astrologers." But as he describes it, "While these winds veered about and tossed my heart hither and thither, the time passed on; but I was slow to turn to the Lord, and from day to day deferred to live in God, and determined not daily to die in myself."

God also brought concerned friends, such as Alypius, across his pathway, who tried to persuade and help him attain a better way of life. He confesses that his problem was basically moral rather than intellectual. "Enthralled with the disease of the flesh, and its deadly sweetness," he writes in graphic language, "I dragged my chain along, fearing to be loosed." Instead of Alypius lifting him up, Augustine pulled his friend down and away from the faith. But in all of this struggle, most of it unknown to his mother, Monica, back home in North Africa, just "held on" in fervent prayer.

Finally Monica braved the perils of a sea voyage and came to live again with her son in Rome

---

You will know the truth, and the truth will set you free. . . . If the Son sets you free, you will be free indeed.   JOHN 8:32, 36

and Milan. She found him "in grievous danger through despair of ever finding the truth." She was not at all surprised that he had finally renounced his cultish fantasies, but, to his surprise, neither was she overjoyed. She would not settle for outward or halfway reformation. She was glad, he reported, "that I was rescued from error, but could not be satisfied, because I had not yet grasped the truth." Calmly, "with a breast full of confidence," she told him that "she believed in Christ that before she departed this life, she would see me a true believer, and a member of the Church."

Monica thought that her son's moral problems might be cured by a proper Christian marriage. For some reason, she did not encourage him to marry the mistress with whom he had lived for almost 15 years, and who had reared his son. He sent this woman back home to Africa, and the son stayed with him in Rome. There Augustine wooed and became engaged to a young girl, who was still two years away from marriageable age. But his sinful habits soon overcame him. He took another mistress and, as he admits, "became even more wretched." Monica, close enough again to sense

---

The prayer of a righteous man is powerful and effective.
JAMES 5:16

the depth of his sinfulness, only increased and intensified her praying.

Augustine was still trying unsuccessfully to climb to salvation and to heaven by what one has called "the flimsy ladder of logic." As he testifies, "I sought a way of acquiring strength sufficient to enjoy God, but I found it not until I embraced that 'Mediator between God and man, the man Christ Jesus,' [who was] calling unto me and saying, 'I am the way and the truth and the life'" (John 14:6).

His major problem was that he still struggled to hold on to his pet sin. "The Way, the Savior himself, was pleasant to me," he confesses. "But as yet I disliked to pass through its straightness" and to follow the "narrow way, that leads unto life eternal." Continued searching and seeking finally brought him to admit his own personal responsibility for his depraved condition. "It was I who willed, who was unwilling," he later admitted; "it was I, even I myself." He was at war within himself. As he went on to describe himself, "I neither willed entirely, nor was entirely unwilling."

For it is by grace you have been saved, through faith—and this not from yourselves, it is the gift of God—not by works, so that no one can boast. EPH. 2:8-9

He said mentally, "Let it be done now, let it be done now." He "all but came to a resolve," he reports. "I all but did it, yet I did it not." His only encouragement was that he did not fall back to his old condition, but "took up my position close by." Surely he was "not far from the kingdom of God" (Mark 12:34).

Complete renunciation and separation from known sin was his final hindrance to saving faith. Those "unruly habits" discouraged him from believing that he could ever live up to the light of the gospel as he now knew it. Then his old habit of procrastination again beset him. He prayed, as too many seekers in every century and culture have pleaded since then, "O God, grant me chastity and purity. But not yet." He was still trying to overcome evil in his own strength, rather than relying on God's enabling grace. The example of many others in that local church successfully living the holy life only added to his misery.

5. *"Take Up and Read"*

Augustine was invited to enjoy a "holiday" retreat at the rural villa of a close friend. He does not tell us if his mother was along, but we know that she was nearby in body and in intercessory prayer. One fateful day he went out into the garden of the villa, along with Alypius. This close friend was also praying for deliverance from sin and faith in the Savior.

There, in what became his "beautiful garden of prayer," Augustine caught a glimpse of the exceeding sinfulness of his sin. He saw his misery, "drawn together and heaped up before the sight of my heart." Then, within his tormented soul, "there arose a mighty storm, accompanied by as mighty a shower of tears."

Perhaps a bit ashamed of his unscholarly emotions, he "stole away from Alypius," appar-

---

We urge you not to receive God's grace in vain. . . . I tell you, now is the time of God's favor, now is the day of salvation.
2 COR. 6:1–2

34

ently realizing that salvation is finally an individual decision, no matter how many others may surround us in prayer. Flinging himself down under a certain fig tree, he "gave full course to my tears." He poured out his heart to God, as he later would testify, "How long, how long? Why not now? Why is there not this hour an end to my uncleanness?"

One can almost feel the power of Monica's intercession of many years in the miracle of divine grace that followed. As Augustine reported it, "I was saying these things and weeping in the most bitter contrition of my heart, when, lo, I heard the voice as of a boy or girl, I know not which, coming from a neighboring house, chanting, and often repeating, 'Take up and read, take up and read.'"

His witness continues, "Restraining the torrent of my tears, I rose up, interpreting it no other way than as a command to me from heaven to open the book, and to read the first chapter I should light upon" (something he never recommended to others as a Bible study method). He quickly returned to where Alypius was sitting, picked up the New Testament scroll, and in silence read what became to him "wonderful words of

---

Faith comes from hearing the message, and the message is heard through the word of Christ. ROM. 10:17

life." The scripture to which he opened was what we now recognize as Rom. 13:13-14. The Bible message was the challenge of the apostle Paul, whose own life had been dramatically changed when he met Christ, many years earlier, on the road from Jerusalem to Damascus. His words spoke directly to the need of this fourth-century prodigal: "Not in orgies and drunkenness, not in sexual immorality and debauchery, not in dissension and jealousy. Rather, clothe yourselves with the Lord Jesus Christ, and do not think about how to gratify the desires of the sinful nature."

In his own descriptive words, "No further would I read, nor did I need: for instantly, as the sentence ended—by a light, as it were, of security into my heart—all the gloom of doubt vanished away." Augustine the searching seeker became Augustine the happy finder.

The excited new Christian testified to his friend, there with him in the garden, and asked him to read the same passage of Scripture. Alypius read Augustine's transforming portion without any impact on his own doubt and unbelief. Then he continued on to the next verse, "Accept him

---

Therefore, if anyone is in Christ, he is a new creation; the old has gone, the new has come!   2 COR. 5:17

whose faith is weak." Augustine rejoiced as his friend, "by a good resolution and purpose, without any restless delay, joined me," as a new believer.

The new converts rushed to find Monica. Augustine's description of her reaction is probably the understatement of the centuries. As he brought to her the glad tidings of his conversion, in his own words, "She rejoiced." Then as he went on to describe how his transformation had come to pass, "She leaped for joy, and triumphed, and blessed God, who was 'able to do exceeding abundantly above all that we ask or think'" (Eph. 3:20, KJV). What a camp meeting celebration it was!

The words of the New Testament Gospel writer may best describe Monica's feelings. We should all empathize with her response, so much like that of the waiting Father of the Bible story of the prodigal son. "We had to celebrate and be glad ... For this son of mine was dead and is alive again; he was lost and is found" (Luke 15:32, 24).

There could be no human yardstick to measure Monica's happiness over her son's amazing transformation. She had known the joy of motherhood 33 years earlier, when she saw her infant

---

For it is with your heart that you believe and are justified, and it is with your mouth that you confess and are saved.
ROM. 10:10

son of promise for the first time. She had watched him respond, and grow, and gurgle his happiness. How much more did she now rejoice in the new birth and new life of this her "son of so many prayers and tears."

Meeting God in that garden had done in a moment of spiritual birth what years of effort and struggle had never been able to accomplish. He still had much of Christian living and of sound doctrine to work through and would spend the rest of his life seeking to "grow in grace, and in the knowledge of [his] Lord and Saviour Jesus Christ" (2 Pet. 3:18, KJV). He would know temptation's power, but now he was assured of victory through God's amazing grace.

In the glory of his newfound joy and peace, he could say, "How sweet did it become to me to be without the delight of trifles. And what at one time I feared to lose, it was now a joy to me to put away. For You, O Lord, cast them away, and instead of them, did enter in yourself, sweeter than all pleasure, brighter than all light, more exalted than all honor. Now was my soul free from the gnaw-

---

Sing and make music in your heart to the Lord, always giving thanks to God the Father for everything, in the name of our Lord Jesus Christ. EPH. 5:19-20

ing cares of seeking and of wallowing and exciting the itch to lust." He could hardly find words to express his gratitude. The cultured teacher of rhetoric and public speaking now testified, "I babble unto You, my brightness, my riches, and my health, the Lord my God."

A vignette from his later *Confessions* gives us a glimpse of a fourth-century family altar. Augustine completed his vacation in the villa with his friend Alypius. He gratefully describes, "My mother clinging to us, in woman's garb truly, but with a man's faith, with the peacefulness of age, full of motherly love and Christian faith." After praying and praising God, he read from the psalms of David, "those faithful songs and sounds which exclude all prideful swelling of spirit, when new to God's true love." The transformed intellectual testifies almost in the language of a camp meeting shout of praise, "I cried out as I read this outwardly and felt it inwardly."

6. *All Is Well*

Augustine, and Monica as well, could never praise God enough for what He had done. In an anthem of praise, he declares, "You, O Lord, are good and merciful, and Your right hand has removed from my heart that abyss of corruption." He now "willed to do what God willed." It was without question the most wonderful holiday, and the beginning of the greatest year of Monica's life. She had rejoiced when her husband was converted and she saw him finally brought into God's fold. Now this son of so many tears and prayers, her black sheep, her personal prodigal, was also safely home. She had lived long enough to see her prayers bountifully answered.

Meeting Christ had done for Augustine, in a moment of spiritual birth, what years of struggle and effort had failed to accomplish. He still had much to learn, even about basic Christian living and doctrine, but he was an apt learner.

Augustine soon wrote to Bishop Ambrose, as a grateful son in the gospel, confessing his former errors and present resolutions. This saintly man of

God helped to disciple and prepare the new Christians to receive Christian baptism and join the church.

Monica had "leaped for joy" when her son shared the details of his newfound faith. We can only imagine her efforts to contain herself on that Easter Sunday in A.D. 387 when he was baptized in the church at Milan. It was certainly another near camp meeting celebration to Augustine himself. He writes of what the service of worship meant to his soul. "How greatly did I drink in the hymns and canticles." He goes on to tell us that he was "deeply moved by the voices of Thy sweet-speaking church. The voices flowed into my ears, and the truth was poured forth into my heart, and my tears ran over, and I was blessed therein."

Monica must also have been delighted that Alypius joined Augustine in thus publicly declaring his faith, as he had in conversion. Adding to her joy, she saw her grandson in the flesh, Adeodatus, now 15 years of age, follow his father in Christian baptism. This son, though "born to me

---

Now to him who is able to do immeasurably more than all we ask or imagine, according to his power that is at work within us, to him be glory in the church and in Christ Jesus through-out all generations, for ever and ever! Amen. EPH. 3:20-21

carnally, of my sin," as he describes it, had chosen to follow his father on the high road of redemption. He was at almost the same age as Augustine was when he chose the low road of rebellion, leading to the far country of sin. Adeodatus never wavered in his faith and helped his father write a helpful book for the young people of their church. He lived only 3 more years, and his father would testify that "I now recall him to mind with a sense of security."

Monica's ministry was not yet ended, now that her prayers for Augustine had been so dramatically answered. She had prayed too habitually for her boy for her to ever stop praising God for His merciful answers. Imperial persecution arose soon after their return to Milan, chiefly against Bishop Ambrose. Many pious people kept guard in the church, prepared to die with their bishop. Augustine reports, "There my mother, God's handmaid, bearing a chief part of these cares and watching, lived in prayer."

God graciously prepared His faithful servant for her soon departure. She confided to her son,

---

Stand firm. Let nothing move you. Always give yourselves fully to the work of the Lord, because you know that your labor in the Lord is not in vain.　　1 COR. 15:58

"My hopes for this world have all been realized. Now, what do I here?" Five days later she was prostrated by fever. Looking up at Augustine, she told him, "Here shall you bury your mother."

Her son knew that Monica's often expressed wish had been to be buried beside her husband, back home at Tagaste in North Africa. This, however, now seemed to be a minor matter to the mature Christian saint. "Lay this body anywhere," she told her son. "Let not the care for it trouble you at all." She had assured several friends that "nothing is far to God; nor do I fear lest He should be ignorant at the end of the world of the place where He is to raise me up."

Augustine made a quick trip to nearby Ostia to arrange for passage back to Africa and home for his mother, himself, and his son. Three years previously, he had stolen away from his mother, a day before his scheduled departure, to meet his destiny in what, at that time, was far distant Italy. Now, when he returned to Milan, he found that his mother had departed the day before for God's better country.

Listen, I tell you a mystery. . . . For the trumpet will sound, the dead will be raised imperishable, and we will be changed.
1 COR. 15:51-52

Augustine had received from his mother an assurance that meant much to him in the trying days of funeral preparation and service. Monica had recalled to him what every person wishes later that he could have heard from his own mother. She told him, with a great display of affection, "that she had never heard any harsh or reproachful sound come out of his mouth against her." This testimony of his love and respect gives us understanding of why he grieved so deeply, in later recalling that he had once "lied to my mother, and such a mother."

Monica had lived 56 years, and her son 33, when, as he writes, "that religious and devout soul was set free from the body." Her funeral service was a victory celebration, with no "tearful plaints and groaning." Her son took comfort in the assurance that "she neither died unhappy, nor did she altogether die." He shed his tears privately. His weeping was not for her homegoing, but for the memory of that mother who was "for a while dead to my eyes, who had for so many years wept for me, that I might live in God's eyes." He recog-

---

Although I am less than the least of all God's people, this grace was given me: to preach to the Gentiles the unsearchable riches of Christ. EPH. 3:8

nized that no honor he could pay her "could be compared with her slavery for me!"

Even before Monica's death, her son had felt God's call to serve as a ministering priest. He had won his friend Alypius to faith in Christ within minutes of his own conversion. As he had prayed and rejoiced with his mother on that never-to-be-forgotten holiday, he declared, "How I was inflamed toward God by those Psalms, and burned to rehearse them, if it were possible, throughout the whole world." He would have that opportunity. He knew that his mother had recognized God's special call upon his life. Augustine spent the next 43 years fulfilling that divine commission.

Monica's son proved that one's weakness can be so divinely reinforced that it becomes an area of strength. In the same way, God uses a man's strong points, his natural gifts and graces, for His even greater glory.

Augustine's love for people, which had once led him into sin and uncleanness, now became a means of winning others to the Christ Monica had loved and served so faithfully. His own bitter and barren experiences, during the years of his rebellion, were used of God to help him understand and encourage others to overcome their particular temptations. In one beautiful analogy, he prayed, "Have pity, O Lord God, lest they who pass by trample on the unfledged bird; and send Thine angel, who may restore it to its nest, that it may live until it can fly."

His accomplished oratory was now put to its highest use in preaching the same gospel that had become for him "the power of God unto salvation" (Rom. 1:16, KJV). His strong talent of leadership brought him to prominence as a bishop in his church in his home area of Hippo in North Africa.

His brilliant mind, which had so long been enmeshed in cultish superstition and error, was now channeled into an intense desire for knowledge and love of truth. In this area, his most lasting influence became the "tongue of his pen." He wrote hundreds of books and articles defending the church against heathen philosophy and practice. His outstanding work, *The City of God,* helped to establish him as perhaps the greatest theologian since the apostle Paul of New Testament days.

His *Confessions* is the record of his sins and struggles and deliverance by God's grace. In this

---

We always thank God for all of you . . . We continually remember . . . your work produced by faith, your labor prompted by love, and your endurance inspired by hope in our Lord Jesus Christ.   1 THESS. 1:2-3

devotional classic, he sought to "awaken my own love and that of my readers toward God, that we may all say, 'Great is the Lord, and greatly to be praised.'"

Amid all the honors heaped upon him, Augustine maintained the same humility and singleness of purpose that had been modeled before him by his mother, Monica. He would testify by his lips and his life that "my desire is not of the earth, nor of gold and silver, and precious stones, nor gorgeous apparel, nor honors and powers, nor the pleasures of the flesh, nor even of necessities for the body."

Monica, a simple, humble, untrained ancient housewife and mother, could not overcome all the negative influence of her husband and the pagan society of her time. She could not convince him of his gross cultish errors. She could not release him from the sensual sins that bound his life for so many painful years. She could not make the desperately needed changes in his heart and life-style.

Monica could only "do her best, and leave the rest" with God. She could train him in the things of Christ and take him to the church she loved

---

But seek first his kingdom and his righteousness, and all these things will be given to you as well.   MATT. 6:33

and served so well. She could love her son unselfishly and unconditionally. Most of all, she could pray, pray with the faithfulness and persistence that must have moved the very heart of God to answer her petitions. In the process, she became one of history's greatest prayer warriors. Through the life of her illustrious son, she influenced her world and future generations for good and for God.

Monica poured out her life in devotion to God and in prayer for her son. She lived like the unnamed New Testament woman who broke an alabaster jar of expensive perfume and poured it on the head of Christ. Jesus defended her actions to the watching critics, saying, "She did what she could. . . . She has done a beautiful thing to me" (Mark 14:8, 6). He went on to promise that "wherever the gospel is preached throughout the world, what she has done will also be told, in memory of her" (v. 9).

Monica well deserves a similar memorial.

Charm is deceptive, and beauty is fleeting; but a woman who fears the Lord is to be praised. . . . let her works bring her praise.   PROV. 31:30-31